Raquel Tanida

The Sun
And
The Star

To order additional copies of this book, contact:
Xlibris
844-714-8691
www.Xlibris.com
Orders@Xlibris.com

ISBN: Softcover   978-1-6641-3602-1
        Hardcover   978-1-6641-3603-8
        EBook   978-1-6641-3601-4

Library of Congress Control Number: 2020920045

Print information available on the last page

Rev. date: 10/14/2020

The Sun
And
The Star

Dedication

I dedicate this book to all kids in the world, specially the ones diagnosed with cerebral palsy, like me.

Once upon a time there was a big sun always lightning the days. His name was Sunlito. He was fun and happy. He liked to rise every morning and show his warmth.

Sunlito warmed the waves in the ocean while he also played with his friends:

Momma Whale, Baby Whale, and Blue Dolphin.

One night, Sunlito was going to sleep and he noticed a beautiful light shining in the sky.

It was Luna, one of the most beautiful stars in the universe.

Luna was a very big and happy yellow star. During the nights, she was always playing with the moon, other planets, and the sisters-stars.

Luna also wanted to play with that big yellow sun in the sky.

But Luna was very shy to introduce herself to Sunlito, and she decided to go sleep.

Sunlito was also very shy to introduce himself to Luna and ask her to play with him in the sky.

What to do?

Sunlito and Luna had a mutual friend. His name was Fluffy, a big, happy cloud that roamed the skies during the day and during the night always happy and singing.

So, Sunlito asked Fluffy if he could help him, and Luna asked Fluffy for help too.

Can help me

YOU?

please?

And Fluffy had a very good idea: he could introduce Sunlito to Luna and everyone could play in the sky together.

One evening, Fluffy waited for Luna arrives in the sky and him introduced her to Sunlito. Then, everyone was happy and started talking.

And since then, every evening, friends get together to play in the sky.

The End.

About the Author

Raquel Tanida was born very prematurely in January 2000, and had a stroke within the first 45 minutes of her life. But she overcomes this challenge and she had a very good childhood.

Raquel graduated from High School in 2018 and today attends classes at the local college in Houston, Texas, where she lives with her parents and brother.

Raquel has always thought about writing a book, but she didn't know what the theme would be. But observing some children, she realized the difficulty that some of them had in relating to each other. And she decided to write about the subject playfully.

This book is intended to help all children who, in some way, feel uncomfortable starting conversations, and how to count on friends for support.

To purchase more copies of this
book, or send you comments and
suggestions, please send an email to:

raquel.tanida@hotmail.com

Printed in the United States
By Bookmasters